Rowell's Run

Poetry and Gleanings
1972 - 1974
Johnny Lyons

Direct inquiries to:
2 Pups Enterprises
PO Box 42
Lecompton, KS 66050

Printed in USA

First printing 2019

ISBN 978-1-7335472-2-2

For Bobby and Bevie

Deepest Thank You to Karla and the Team at
"2 Pups Publishing"
for Making the Dream come true.

The Backstory

These pieces were found among the journals I kept
from 1971- 1974.
Within those years, I attended and graduated from
Brockport SUNY   (in Upstate New York) with a
B.A. in British and American Literature.
As a Folk-singer, I performed regularly in Pizza
Parlors, Bars and Coffee-houses on
campus and off. Getting paid to play and
sing – truly in my Stride.
I mainly hung out and played at
The Crypt Coffeehouse in the cellar of
St Luke's Episcopal church- built in the 1850's-
truly a "crypt".
It Was "The Scene" and the Hottest place in
town,
with the Best Vegetarian kitchen.
Run by students, it was a magnet for those of us
who had alternative and progressive
viewpoints, we became close and dear friends.
Musicians, writers, poets, playwrites, actors,
directors, dancers and clowns
The Food was Great, the Music was Great, the
Conversations and Ideas were Great
There was I smack-dab in the middle of it all.

Connections began to be made with people on
"The Commune Circuit"
Texas – Arkansas – Vermont – Virginia

- New York -

We visited other "Communes" and they visited us.
we grew, we evolved, we grew closer and our
dreams multiplied.
Then we decided to buy a farm and get back to the
land.
live, work, play, love
Soon, ten of us moved in together at the "Utica
House",
We Planned, Searched through Realty /Land,
catalogues,
We Researched Chickens, Ducks, Birds and Bees,
Milk Cows, Goats, Farming,
Gardening, Fruit Trees, Composting
We all were Young, Excited and Eager to build the
Vision.

I'd never seen a mule or milked a cow in my life.
The Foxfire Books, Whole Earth Catalogue and
Mother Earth News were Bibles

We Dreamed and Worked and Saved. We pooled
our earnings with the rule:

"Nobody lives on the Farm until it's paid for."

In the Fall of '72 we found a 300 acre farm in West
Virginia for $13,500.

Rowell's Run
March 1973
population: 12 and growing
p.s. No Electricity, No Plumbing

The only camera I had was the nib of my pen.

This is what you shall do: Love the earth and sun and animals, despise riches, give alms to everyone that asks, stand up for the stupid and the crazy, devote your income and labor to others, hate tyrants, argue not concerning God, have patience and indulgence toward the people, take off your hat to nothing known or unknown or to any man or number of men, go freely with powerfull uneducated persons and with the young and with the mothers of families, read these leaves in the open air every season of every year of your life, re-examine all you have been told at school or church or in any book, dismiss whatever insults your own soul and you very flesh shall be a great poem and have the richest fluency not only in words but in the silent lines of its lips and face and between the lashes of your eyes and in every motion and joint of your body.... The poet shall not spend his time in unneeded work. He shall know that the ground is always ready plowed and manured... Others may not know it but he shall. He shall go directly to the creation. His trust shall master the trust of everything he touches... and shall master all attachment.

The known universe has one complete lover and that is the greatest poet.

Walt Whitman
Prologue - LEAVES OF GRASS

"Whitman, Walt. *Leaves of Grass*. Brooklyn, NY. 1855"

1972

Sepia Scratches

and it's very strange to me to
know how to write with a new pen-
in your brown- eyed colour
Sepia...

my line is too drifting for
words to speak.
Brown-eyed Sepia coloured wind
fine print pen barely touches paper
scratch scratch the rocks
that make the wall, symbols
sent high through starry atmosphere
blue organic origins.
faint lines make even shadows
from the light of stars and the
moon - in all its wright
No wind blows ~ ~ ~ ~ ~
It was the sea...those many years ago
– it was La Mer
it was she, who with delicate
breath of oyster shell and wind,
fin and coral rock,
between... shore and water that brought her-
the moon within our distant and dilating vision.

The pine moon shadows too did
call out on the February night
from hillsides wanting to be
born.
Those first pine-moon shadows
that startled the owl and the buck
The calm instant comprehension that followed...
From the etchings on rock, their shadows not
gathered-
only information on a page.
Questions asked.
Rather   an instant reflecting comprehension
Scratches in Sepia.

Jwl 1972

A March Poem

The sun becomes brighter
   The sky blu'er
   and only a few clouds
hovering high in the distance
   Horizons

Notice how longer the days become
   even the sun seems larger than
   it was, or

Is it that my eyes are wider?
   Or my height taller?

jwl 1972

Becoming the Horizon

It began to rain today, instead of snow
        to see raindrops in brown street puddles
make round circles and floating bubbles
           that the wind sails to the edge,
then burst like the ending of something
                becoming the horizon.

Jwl 1972

Swelled Roots

Peeling and Cutting
Potatoes for supper meal.
Think of the Karma around un-peeled Potatoes.
True Enlightenment in a swelled root
from underneath wet, brown earth.

All my people who depended
upon that swelled
root.
Eire
The Stone and Thatch, The Draping Mists,
The Rivers Lee, The Blackwater and The Bandon
flow south from the Galtee and Shehy mountains.
To the East ~
~Araglin and Comeragh Mountain ranges.
Then Sea.

An Gorta Mor
Dark Famine Shadows linger still.

We family, become that swelled root
that wet earth
that underneath soil,
That Hunger.
We family, become that struggle
to etch and scratch our lives from beneath
Copperplated Earth.

I eat the last potato crumbs
at the border of my plate,
that sit like soft white mountains
in the near distance.

jwl 1972

Windy Vegetable Soup

Saturday September 16, '72
A very beautiful day with strong, strong
wind ~ a lot of sunshine ~ I made vegetable
soup ~ all from the garden and it certainly
is magic ~ The wind got very strong as I
climbed into bed and 'think it will rain
tonight.

The wind sends eddies of airy wind
through and around the walls of this room
~ the curtains move gently in and out.
Some images:
-when the tree joins the earth
-inside where the shadow falls
-at the beginning of a river
even at the first drop of
water that rolls.
-Some fodder for poetry....
I think the wind symbol is important
today, so I will read the i-Ching/Wind
symbol before I sleep.
I feel very good today – it has grown nicer
with every movement I made.

Jwl 1972

The house most peaceful
most good in the silence
like night snowfall
my spirit glides through every
snow dripped windowpane,
walls cold, not damp.
Oaken floors creak where we've walked
A song of every corner in the house.

Jwl 1972

The Baby Cries at Three in the Morning

The baby cries at three in the morning
        and others dance in far away lands.
             light footsteps cross floorboards above
How moves my hand at this hour?
Words and languages overflow
        from Spirit Well to Hand

Sense the Light at my feet
        and the backside of the Universe
             Immense,   Thick
        like Syrup in Amber Colored Jars.

The baby cries at three in the morning
        and soothed by the mother's hand
             warm,
          under pulled back covers.

Cold night air chills my feet to head,
Spinal Frost that tingles to finger's end
I write, numbed on by night's cold.

Body warmth keeps it's boundary inside.

What is it that moves this pencil lead across White
Wood?
Write with Rock across the Earth
White across Brown,
Mushroom ink smeared on fingers
Black across Green Grass,
Grey pencil scratches across White Wood.

The baby sleeps.

Jwl 1972

Half Banked Sleep

Words and letters that need to be writ'
    Crusts and orange peels for the morning
        ....Will wake at dawn's light

        "The Potato Poem" they said.
    I know the magic there in those roots
            and bulbs and tubers
                Strong Magic

        Rolling over in half~banked sleep,
            The blown out lamp
        A quiet darkness rests here

jwl 1972

Prob'ly Henry Thoreau sat
cross-legged in the grass
hands folded on his knee
laughing with the sun.

On summer nights
listening to the stars move
Sack-cloth clothes
hang fluently in an August wind,

Supposing that the fair earth
were but a reflection
of the eye

jwl 1972

The twinkling stars tonight
  empty boughs
  make them twinkle more.

The -more than half - moon
  unlike the day
  so very bright.

Winds settle here, then lift
  through the boughs
that make the stars twinkle more.

Grey mists grew hovery deep thick clouds
  though the afternoon
  making it tedious to walk.

When I didn't walk,
I might remember this day
as one spent sanding an old oaken chair,
and my words begin to
cramupagainsteachother
that this might end up to look like the sea
as waves get closer to the shore.

I wish I somehow could remember the names of
days

jwl 1972

Sunday night October 8 1972

The pages turn. This weekend seven
of us drove down to West Virginia
saw a farm (after 3 flat tires)
and I fell in love – it was unanimous
we made the decision and began the steps
to buy it. 300 or so acres, $13,000
(we have 75% in the bank right now) hills –
woods
 2 houses, Big Barn and several out bldgs –
chicken coop, above ground 2 story
food cellar, grain bin. All in decent shape...
just needs up- dating and tlc..
No Running Water, No Electrity, I'm
bursting!

Jwl 1972/2019

Pencil makes mem'ry,
like John in the wilderness
cries out for one true vision
and being insane.

With all these visions of land
and horses and the sacred buffalo
The one truest lies further
in towards the heart
and it is hard to touch the
tree- tops from upon the land
without becoming the tree

A present vision is fifteen people wide
I have become those people
and likewise the vision.

Jwl 1972

If our movements flow
    like rainfall on the rooftop
        Then I may catch you in my hand

These nights have been too lonely
These days
I spend like money
And come home

If our movements flow
    like rainfall on the rooftop
        Then I may catch you in my hand

jwl 1972

**Wednesday, Sometime in May
a few hours into Thursday.**

How the house,
at night lies still
        without a sound
in the growing warm womb
        toes say they are cold

Aren't we all making love?
When the times sometimes
even make it hard sometimes

The candle is very bright
        when once at first lit
                Grows dim deep shadows
                from the hedge across the way.
Building ever brighter,
the candle must realise
        it is the only light
that burns within the house.

        Sip the milk
    Fall asleep asking for visions
Fall asleep not asking for rain

Aren't we all making love?

1973

March 31, 1973

A 500 mile, two day journey
South from Brockport
through the Southern Tier of New York State.

The Genesee River – Springville Town and the
Cattaraugus Creek.

Chautauqua Lake to the Allegheny National Forest,
and into Pennsylvania.

The land seems to rise and form Hills and Ridges
before our eyes.
Like a rumpled blanket.

We skirt Pittsburgh.

Into West Virginia and All Points South to
Morgantown
Hwy.79 - heading for Calhoun County, Grantsville,
Creston, and the Little Kanawa River.

From there,
it's Narrow Dirt Roads, Switchbacks,
Tree'd Hillsides, Small Farmhouses
the Occasional Gardens, Humans, Horses, Dogs
And the Too Occasional "One Arm Bandit" oil
wells.

"You don't "move" to West Virginia...
you screw yourself in."

A mile or so of more dirt road, turns to a creek-
bed for a bit

Tucked back in

The Holler they call **Rowles Run**

300 Acres of Home

April 7, 1973 Saturday

Jonathan, Rona and I arrived here on our farm a week ago, with a truckload of supplies.

After exploring the property- buildings etc - the first tasks:

clean the "big" house so it's Livable and work on the well:

15 feet down – stone walls – had to bail it out, Jonathan & I taking turns-

down the ladder, haul up bucket of old water – dump .... over & over.

We hit the muddy bottom, found old broken cups, whiskey bottles, critter bones and a spoon.

...cleaned it out- best we could - let it fill – in the meantime, built a

wooden plank cover for it and
support for the hand pump.

Once we got it set, it was pump
and dump for three cycles-

adding a gallon of bleach each cycle...

The Cookstove set up and functioning in
the kitchen,
Elmer – the Pot-belly stove set in the center
of the living room

having a love affair with stovepipe is a
challenge

Neighbor Marion comes Monday to plow
the first garden

it's so quiet

A strong stream bank Sabbath evening, rainbow to the east.

Yellows, Blues, Reds. A strong stream bank
evening, up in the holler wood.
Unrecognizable from when I last passed through
~they too, the woods, have changed and grown
very green
 Hands and knees in the water, like deer for drink.
        Tree-tops reflected, the world in a tiny pool.

It rained a few hours and now the rain stopped,
        trees drip rain.
    birds sit silent for a spell~
        far off
the Pileated Woodpecker sends forth her cry
homeward.

Disappated green light filters the evening
shading to dim dusky green as the sun moves
farther west.
        The wind brings more tree rain~
                a medicine wheel
Of wood trees green, of dripping water,
        of a strong stream
        and of the birds that dwell within the wood.

The Waiting

May Apple, shiny leaf   mandrake root
What four legged animals live up here?
Perhaps
deer ~ doe, buck, fawn
A chipmunk
scurrying.
A raccoon waking
A squirrel that waits for nuts.
The fox that waits
for the squirrel.

I wait, then head for home

It is well.

May 7, 1973

   spent the day with Bill Cumings and Fred Hayes from the Forest Service, touring the property, learning "forest and land management".

Areas have been "logged" in the past – huge swathes on the hillsides cleared and now making a recovery.

Probably for Black Walnut trees – Big Money.

   the terrain of the hillsides makes it difficult for "large scale" clearing. (thank God)

I kept a list of all the species of trees we have- 16 in all

Shagbark Hickory – Red Maple - White Oak – Ash – Tulip Tree - Beech – Sugar Maple – Gum - Pitch Pine - Sassafrass – Red Oak – Virginia Scrub Pine – Scarlet Oak - Chestnut – Black Oak – Sumac – Red Cedar and Black Walnut

May 12,1973

In Japan, the Dragonfly is believed to be the Incarnation of Ancestor Spirits who dwell beside the village. I have noticed and watched many- here along the bottom of hills and banks of streams. Shy and aloof creatures, for they will not alight on your hand. However, if you follow one, they will pickup on your energy and seem to watch you as well, with a gentle and curious gaze.

Alone in the center
     of a wide circle
Pebble in a Stream
     The waves issued
– backwash cleansing
No breezes stirring

Songs lifting up to Heaven
     Doe and fawn
Drink at the stream
Whipoorwills have no nest
     A day-bed for deer
Lamplight. Lamplight.

Summer 1973

The FBI and Sheriffs Dept. came by today,
looking for Walter Cronkite's daughter
who's been kidnapped.
                    Really.
            Pretty weird and scary – but they
            were nice
            No girls with mustaches here ! Sorry.

May 18,1973
Early West Virginia Morning
        heavy misty fog in the valley.

                Breakfast on the cookstove –
                        muffins with berries
        I picked this morning in the back holler
on The Morris Farm.
                Freshly churned Butter,
                still warm milk, from the milking.

                Before supper meal
                The day turned into an extremely hot
and torrid day. Lenny
disc'd in 2 acres of peas that went to seed
early.

                        Another Grande influx of
people to our farm. Caroline came home
finally from a Texas visit with her folks, 2
other friends from Brockport, and 3 others
I don't know.

        I think on the transient aspect of
these times and how it filters down and
manifests to us here on the farm.
                It's a Constant Presence, this
                Human Flow.
                        This Searching, this Curiosity.

Even Egyptians broke plough handles

Cow Milk Scratches

working the farm
bigoldmare to pull the truck from the mud
                        again.
Rain, Rain
splashing the ground.
Puddles and Frogs Eggs like Rotted Rope
laying by the roadside.

Dewy mornings when mists veil the hillsides
Nights when the sky clears and bright stars spread
                        Lao Tsu
Hopi dance migration like a herd of a thousand
buffalo.

Towhee calling through the Pitch Pine
            answer from the Cedar Grove
Apple Wind smell, Deer trail and Fresh tracks.

Cow milk scratched in a tin bucket foaming
        Bright White from Green Grass.

Red Spring Buds on High Up Trees.
Turkey
      wild
            in the wood
calls upon the morning ridge.
Snail shell in a creekbed,
Cowbirds, Towhee, a Charm of Gold Finches.
            Mallard duck in the gardens.

Sunday

Planting squash, in-between
Rows   ,   of   ,   corn
In hills five or six   seeds
Once in, below the soil and sun – yellowed sky,
Some Norwegian seaweed

      Whippoorwill and fireflies
Looking at maps and thinking of traveling

Fresh golden straw for the bed
      All books in a pile
Blackberry and Rhubarb pie
      Re-reading Walden

Pages and pages, always turning

The Earth always turning

You can be Joyful, Knowing what you are

Scurry Beetle across the mat

Whippoorwills stop singing

Frogs in the valley hushed

Summer Solstice near Seven Days

You can be Joyful, Knowing what you are

Watercircles

There is balance
of green, red and brown.
The birds that fly. The insects that fly too, and
crawl as well.
The rotted fallen tree. The cracked stump
that still stands watch.
The spirit of rain and too, the rain that falls from
leaves
After Rain Reflections in the pool from where I
drink
The aroma of wet forest in Spring growing
and of last years growth that rests there too.

Spirit of Worldly Life, the Green and the Flesh
Spirit and the Wheel.
Dripping rain like a thousand footsteps above
drops watercircles on the page

The larger brook in the distance away
that I must cross

jwl/1973

All connexions – this still summer night
no Whipoorwill and many silent Fireflies.
A dusky glow from kerosene lamp and the faint

pencil line trace.
No sound from the open window.
How strange from the previous nights,
when the woods would come alive with nocturnal
sound.

An expectation of storm.
Fill fill fill the page
Stillness
Sensibilities to the external forces,
within as well as without.
The day ruled by Mars.
But now, no disagreement
among the sleeping bodies.
What day tomorrow?
Mercury

the ribbon

a tiny campfire in wooded darkness
    valley echoes of my people

pot of cold creek water
    spice-bush branch and leaf for tea

    ribbon braided in my hair

faint stars speak of constellations
    and hazy clouds

the air gets colder, night dew falls
    and embers drift

With Ed Powell

July 3 Wednesday 1973

Yesterday I was talking with a new friend Ed Powell from the University of Buffalo, Bobby Minkoff's Sociology professor.

He asked me if anyone was making a journal of the farm- a written record of the things that happen here and how how really important it could be.
Not only to "Us", but to other people, our children as well.

Like any new notion, it takes a "head-change" - another view or perspective, realizing the "Here and Now" is only important in terms of the past and future.
All is a Continual Stream.

I know how fascinated by old photographs of people and places I've been. Without a camera, and given my natural faculties, I may serve as an Organic Camera – with all the wrinkles and lines, feelings and odors and colors and sounds.
Alive inside the photograph.

July 4th Afternoon 1973

More half-inch July rains ~ July 4
-    the day Thoreau moved to Walden Pond.

loving someone as warm as the July sun
    flowers grown under her care

sweet smell of fresh cut hay

field corns mark light green rows
  over wet brown soil
green lines on brown parchment
filled in by a runaway poem

climbing beans that hadn't been there in the
morning

touch and breath that I call mine

Waterwind

Greening reflections swim the waters
        it is   The Waterwind
           I watch
      while little eddies of air
         brist my surfaces.

All is silent ~
        for the birds, for the crickets,
for the Earth Damp-smell, ancient fresh

Trees begin to rust, the green steps
             into deeper shadows.

Rust begins at the tree-top

     I sense last hours
drifting in the Waterwind.

The Mexican- Blanket people have
finally left
(for God knows how long)
and the farm is nearing what can be called
"The Wintering In".
In two weeks, three or four more
people will leave and the same number will
be left – Three or four of us.
It's an un-burdening feeling,
so few people living here ~ an un-
complicated period of time.
It feels good to be up here in my
space, watching all the folks
come and go.
I feel much like the hills... just watching

Autumn Birthday

Autumn colors tint your hair
this Autumn Season of Your Birth
Or is it You,
Who tints the World in Your Colors
and Autumnal blessings

jwl 1973 / 2019

Pinto Bean Pick Saturday September 15

Finally the days have been warm and dry enough to start the bean harvest. They were planted around tipis of sapling poles over two acres. All we had to do was up- root the plants, pick up the bean tipi plants and all, lay them down in the row. I'd drive the Team, get the wagon loaded and haul them to the truck. We're storing them in Marion's barn to dry. We'll have all winter to shell and clean and eat.

.... 'told Marion we'd barter all the gas he'd like.

For Judy

I

Perhaps you are a touch of wind
Given me from a western star,
to play on my back and shoulders
and tousle my hair.

I see you by the banks of the stream,
stooping low to bathe your face in the Autumn
waters
  ~all the colored leaves reflected in your eyes.
Doe-prints in the sand from where you step.
Underneath the arching Oak,
        down there by where you bathe.

A soft murmur in the nighttime dark
        warm underneath
                 laying soft.
Touch my hand to your hip,
   another murmur in blanket words
       you move and turn.

It is what makes me say   I Love You.
   Those doe- prints in the sand,
      Those echoes on the walls,
   Those murmurs and turnings.

I begin to see your face with the dawn,
      light touching chin and cheekbone.
the feel of us within each other
      as the light spreads.

II

Clothes hang empty on the cold wooden walls.

I burn a candle for you
  while you are gone,
Chopped and stacked wood,
Built blazing fires
and saw your echoes dancing in the shadows.

Horses out in pasture
        and being alone with you not here.
Carrying my longing-ness
        like a breeze on my back.
  I see you riding on the highway.

Sleep and the not being able to sleep.
Counting breaths in the chilled Autumn air.

Holding something precious and alive

        I hear our love   youme

and the rain drums and patters patterns on the
tin roof,
    kerosene lamp sputters.

Calling Autumn by her first name.

Listen for you coming up the path beside the field
of corn.

III

You are the Seasons to me,
when our eyes meet in the Wood
and the Stream runs by.

You become the Stream sometimes too,
when I pull you up to me,
look in your Mirrors
and see the Seasons.

IV

Autumns First Name

Hiding like the Grouse in the wood.
Sounding like the foot-fall of approaching rain.

I think, it was not the rainfall I heard,
but my Pencil Markings for you.

jwl 1973

Corn shocks in the field
      look like
      Tai Chi dancers
            pushing with the wind

      Tai Chi dancers in the field
      look like
      Corn shocks
            pushing with the wind

jwl 1973/2019

A Sunset and Rembrandt Etchings
Creston Town

The sky had been blue
    and placed behind a wall of October.
Streets hammered on through the day
      Pigeons sat on steeples
or flew down beside where I walked along
    in October Gold.
A chill in the air, leaves settle to ground.

Should it be these squares of concrete gray
    or Patches of Green Ground
    or even the Bark of Trees
where the Leaves might rest , or bounce , or run
      The pigeons have choice.
    Leaves and I have none today
until the time I turned those falling leaves into
    Pages of Rembrandts Etchings at Sunset

Frosted Morning

Milking Cow mornings
drinking fresh warm
body warm milk
after each morning milking
from the pail

- a Norwegian morning
the mountains and valleys
sing a Fjord song
so sweet that song comes to me
Mists rising in the Heat of the Morning sun

October 15, 1973

We had a meeting tonight about spaces, fantasy plans and winter trips.
If all thoughts become reality, there'll only be a handful here, to tend to the farm and creatures – myself included.
My plan is to remodel the up-stairs of the grain-shed.
The need for some private space is very strong and I see it can become a good and peaceful center from where I may be able to continue to develop the Journals and Poetry.

I also can build the Library. The rain is steady.

~~~~

October 13 1973 Saturday

It rained and rained tonight, on our
wheat field - valleys and ridges streams
are noisy full.
Now, All is still,
faint light, over full moon light
underlacing the layers of clouds.
Restful,
until early morning when we will rise,
search out the feed bucket, walk to the
barn, dig into the oats and corn
find Chocolate our Swiss milk girl and her
udders full. But that is tomorrow now it is
nightime- very late.
The night crickets make sounds
like the stars make light.
The hooded warblers four, that we
spied the day before, in the brush,
gathering seed - the males feeding the
females - are silently asleep.
Gooseberrydown.

A woolen vest buttoned twice. Kerosene
lamp turned brighter.
Stronger shadows, slower wordsdrawn
carefully across this page.
Gather bright orange Hickory leaves
tomorrow
     (for they are not as orange tonight in
     the dark air
      where the stand of Hickory stands,
    and the slices of Hickory hull,
      lie like pieces of a Hickory moon)

Shagbark Mockernut Gooseberry down
Find the Hickory nut hulls laying on the
ground.

Potato Dig tomorrow
Corn Harvest Friday
Work Union to finish New Chicken Coop
and Run Saturday

Chant November
November Blue Skies
above the cold foggy morning
Clouds white mist rising
Valley smoke   steel blue

Strong Spirit Wind   New Day Moon
White and Crescent above the Ridgeline
Startled Grouse flies yonder
   asks for softer stepping
on half dried leaves blowing
Crisp and Tumble
   underneath the Soft Pine

Chant November

Cross Tracks

Standing in the cross tracked
               powder snow
Brown shafts of field
               bend frozen
pointing in the direction of the wind.

Turn me to the East
        as I come from the North West ,
           bending frozen
      in the direction of the wind.

Crossing rabbit tracks from the south
     that hop to the bush to smell and return

Cross Tracking in the powdersnow
      like the pattern of snowfall
        on a still
      and shining night.

One Mile from the Farm

Empty pages yet to run
Images hang like clothes on the line
it snows, close now to January
and a New Year

Kanawa river runs one mile from the farm
Wide and Deep the river runs
One mile from the farm

Let the chickens loose!
Open up the barn
Have a feast,
One mile from the farm.

SONGS

There's a couple a apples

On a couple a trees
We're in the heat of the summer weather
Corn needs hoein'
Hay needs mowin'
And we're all hopin' for a heifer.

Well, the spinach is up
And the broccoli too
We got all the fields done and hoed
But we got in trouble
Done burst our bubble
'caught skinny dippin' in the road..

Well it weren't very serious
Tho' Orris got delirious,
He's the man that brings the mail
We just tried to explain, it just ain't the same
To take a bath in an old milk pail.

We're just livin' on the farm
Not doin' no harm
Just tryin' to help the gardens grow
And if you wanna come see,

What it's like to be me,
Just come along and bring a hoe.

(ch)
There's a couple a apples
On a couple trees......

Breughel *

> Snow on the grasses,
> love and wood-ashes
> wind through the pine trees,
> patches on my knees
>
> Blue smoke arisin'
> don't find it surprisin'
> smoke ain't all that
> heavy y'know

Takin' my time by the wood~burnin' stove
warmin' my toes by the warmth of the glow
Glad it ain't summer, summer will come
Spring will come lately, and the day's almost done

> Breughel could capture
> the horse in the pasture
> old cock he crows 'n
> streams are all frozen

Out on the front porch, to gather some wood
rememb'ring places where we once stood
Sundown is sure now, fire and wood
Your arms around me and the feelin' is good

* Pieter Breughel - 16th Century Flemish painter

Horse-drawn Livin' On the Farm (Song)

Dolly and Jack* are pullin' on the wagon
Bob is bringin' up the rear
Sure feels good to be livin' on the land
Bein' this time of year

Chorus:

   O, the Wagon wheels roll
   it's good to roll slow
   Horse~drawn livin' on the farm.
   Stove~wood pilin' up to the sky'n
   I feel a lot of love for you

You're visiting the city,
   where things ain't so pretty,
exceptin' for the smile that you wear.
It gets kinda lonesome
alone in the home-spun
but 'cha know it ain't too 4hard to bear.

Chorus:

   O, the Wagon wheels roll
   it's good to roll slow
   Horse~drawn livin' on the farm
   Stove~wood pilin' up to the sky'n
   I feel a lot of love for you

When you come back
I'll be standin' in the backyard
addin' to the tall wood pile.
I'll throw down my hatchet
close the door and latch it,
and Feast on your Beautiful Smile.

Chorus

jwl 1974

* Dolly was the draught horse, Jack and Bob were mules. Bob was the scrawny one (and my Dad's name)

1974

April Times

I remember these times, April Spring times
how the design has thrust and grow
Sassafrass bud and pollinating Pine

Under the Cedar
to peruse swift days, marching by in succession.

April days are as important as the Whippoorwill
call up the holler,
as lighting the fire in mornings
when the frost is too harsh
    yet the afternoon sun burns hotter than July.

Readying more ground for planting.

Important are the silent buds on the waking trees
and Frost says "Not Yet"

watering horses and mules and milk cow
and to their feeding
watching the slate colored Junco pass by
travelling north for Summer Season
Not to stay to May

    Feeling these April Times

Clearings

Pasture   Hedgerows

Forgotten   Fence-lines

Sting of Barbed Wire

"of course it's rusty …. need to ask?"

Leaning fence posts sunk deep

" … you sure this is our land ?"

Laundry Day

means hours in the Laundromat in town
needs must, when there's children plus 12
adults
Everyone wants to go to town –
"I'll stay if you bring me some beer"

Hours and loads later, word came
"they're back"

Drove the team and wagon to pick
everyone and everything up from the
parking spot. (We don't want cars and
trucks driving up and down the road, so
we made a parking lot of sorts by the turn
to Gordy's place.)

It's such a transition from automobile
to horse and wagon –
Peaceful Easy Pace
although the driver needs to pay attention.
"Now Dolly, get on over there – don't
wanna drive off the road...Now Hup Jack
you're sleepin again"
"Gee Dolly- watch your step - that's a girl.
"C'mon C'mon C'mon   All in a line
now - that's it
Easy Now Whoa Up"

Without women, children and clean
laundry on the wagon,

I pride myself on
Driving the Team and rolling a smoke at
the same time.

Time-Warp in June

I have no real idea of what concrete number
   is on this day.

But,

I know that it is near the end of June.

July is coming, stretching down the holler.

June has been rain and lightning
and lightning and rain.

Sound of strong water flowing the creek-beds.

  Last of the New Greens ready to Deepen Greens

The Oatfield

How beautiful is the Oat Field.

All the stalks turned Golden
after last nights rain,

The Earth turned to deep shades of brown.

I watched the field for a while this morning

then walked through it,

from road to stream.

Such a Gold and Brown!

The vibrations of the soil were of the two colors.

Laying our treasures in the Earth, rather than on.

The Luminescence of Gold can never compare

with the Richness of this soil.

I met an interesting man today

Vern is the Shoemaker in Glenville
          very full, long beard
wide, thin friendly mouth

His shop in leathery tangles
          the air breathes shoes

Turtle Dove Saturday

...got some important things done.
Was warm-hazy and pleasant. Fetched
Dolly (draft mare) from Gordy's pasture,
harnessed her up to the sled piled with tools
and lunch. Ken Dubie's 10 year old son
Robin & I sledded down the road to
Polling's Pasture to fix the Water-Gaps on
the fence line.
It was fun to teach him how to drive
the mare.
A Water- Gap is when the fencing
crosses a stream – and you need to prevent
the stock from ducking underneath the
fence to make their get-away- a real pain
in the ass and it can be a difficult job.
At dusk we cultivated a bean field-
under a beautiful sunset sky.

Any work I do with the horses & mules
makes me very high, brings me so much
closer
 and in touch with the earth so brown.
Rain is needed.
I heard a Turtle Dove this evening
a 3 day sign for rain.

At Leaf's Edge

It showered a bit last night, yet the earth is still pale brown.

Looking forward to fencing the back pasture for our new milk cow ~ Georgia & calf ~ they need the Clover and Orchard grass   helps the calf's growth too....
  Tomorrow taking the teams off Gordy's pasture and onto Polling's for a while.
        Just learned the term "Guttation" - when there is too much water in the plant and water is forced out the vein ends of the leaf forming dots of water at leaf's edge.

There is a smile that rises
above the hill
and pauses above the windowsill

White lace curtain
hangs like first snow fall
Summer to winters green

Calico dress
drops to the floor
Oaken smell of winter
lingers through the open door

Wild Mule from Strawberry Hill and the Mule Whisperer

This week is big "Garden Union Week"
cleaning up the gardens, bean-bug garden
squash parties yesterday and today,
Strawberry Hill hoed and runners set.

I was in the grain shed this afternoon,
when I heard the fast tracks of a Wild
Mule bolting down the road
        the shouts and yells of people in the
                fields
            - a riderless mule.
Jack- the biggest (and smartest)- was
                spooked.
He got away from Frank at Strawberry
        Hill - 2 miles away.
    And he was comin' for Me

He took the backwoods road where trucks
            can't go
    crossing over Cunningham Ridge
        past the little house
    past the startled "bug- pickers"
            past the barns
past the shouting people on the road

I just called his name- arms outstretched
        holding an ear of corn
            we're calm now

White Locks

white locks and a runaway sun
                              in lacy jags.
Planted more seed,
fixed fences.
July sun so hot,
from so far away,
dried the stream bed.
Had to go to the well,
water reaching fifteen foot deep down,
cold as deep winter snow.
My back and shoulders now
Brazen like bronze,
Striped colors on the chipmunks back.

The Characters of my Pockets

I thought today of the various Characters
of my Pockets,

how they take on the Collection of the days'
work and play.

Nails- straight, bent, fence and horseshoe,

Matches, Rolling papers, Tobacco pouch
and Tobacco crumbs,

The "K55" Carbon knife.

Wing feathers, Soft stones. Guitar picks.

It's impossible to carry a "Constant
Charm",
for the pockets go through so many changes
through a day.

The one constant on the farm
is that my pockets rarely carry money
- that feels good.

The rain is steady and I want to nap before
dinner.

Cultivator Jack

This afternoon, Robert was out cultivating the sweet corn with Jack the Mule. He took a siesta in the shade and let Jack graze a little.

I was in the big house and caught a glimpse of our "wild mule"   tearin' up the gravel road … cultivator clangin' behind. Jack ran straight to the barn for his stall and would've made it – but the cultivator caught at the door.

… a few minutes later, Robert came tearing down the road in mad pursuit

- on a bicycle.

Panting and nervous he said:

"I just dozed off a little – I woke up and saw Jack walkin' down the road …. I hollered WHOA MULE – that's all it took. Jack took off as fast as butter lasts around here"

Twice in 4 days is a record.

Now Jack graduates to

The Best Tied-up Mule in Calhoun County.

Saturday - Full Moon

Walking back from singing songs at The Dreamers
farm.
               Full Moon – Orb shining,
         filling the valley with Milk-light
        Hoot Owl calls the Screech Owl
answers from my left   response from my right
  Positive Light through Ringing Moon-shadows
Come now, August's End, High Pitch of Summer
Most growth is done ~
Ripening fruits supply the course of the sun.
Saps stand second-ly still
in the last of Summer's labour.
Land-tides
    "Pull direct there, moon"
    rigging lines pulled taught
~we robust and lusty people
Our children,
Our children, asleep beneath the moon's tide-pull,
turn soft in sleep
and heave a breath in astonished dreams.
Our people, trav'ling courses seemed fit
and Far-off from the Gardens and Forests.

Some to the West   Some to the East
        for another kind of work.
The Season's work pre-ordained,
No Travel needs here.
  Needs ~ only succession and progressions

We talk of space changes and preparing our food
We talk of friends, and scenes that
        passed like water through our senses
    and ideas come forth like hill-side springs
        when the ground is full.

The Song is sung,
A child is nursed, while dishes get washed in the
other room.

Monday September 9 1974

I was awakened this morning at 5a.m. With news- Eloise has gone into labor. A new child to be borne today.

We gathered down to the Tipi, and by 2p.m. Shawnee Jed arrived.
Eloise and Josh are beaming and proud parents
We All Are

Sunday in September 74

I have what appears to be Poison Oak on
my arms -legs – face
   aw hell... all over.
My right eye is totally swollen and shut
   – Blind - One Eyed Poet, am I
We were working a Wood run with the
team up on Cunningham Hill - where there
was an old logging trail. I've never had an
allergic reaction to anything before.
   I was more concerned on how in Gods
name was I going to
drive the team DOWNHILL -
    dragging big logs behind,
   and how to avoid disaster every
inch of the way for me and the team.
  We successfully made three trips –
enough fire wood for at least a week.
   Enough Poison Oak for a lifetime.
   Now I spend time healing myself
with herbs from the same woods.
   Jewel Weed and White Oak Bark teas
and washes.
   Full Circle and Pure Misery

September 25,1974

Rather a scattered day – folks over and off tending to daily tasks and tie-ing rope ends. Later this afternoon
*   Another Bean-bug- Smash party....*
Several Praying Mantises were found among the bean-pods
*   Good Sign.*
Began work on the Grain Shed today.
Copying Poetry tonight under a Quarter moon, yellow and grande out in the valley.

My Desk   74

No matter how I try, my desk is always
in a kind of chaos.
>Strewn papers, matches, pieces of
>rope, broken pencils, ink pens
>a bag of smoke, two knives, couple of
>dollars, tape
>Three books: a Dictionary of
>Symbols,
>>Websters Word Dictionary Dad
>>sent me and Leaves of Grass.
>On the shelf, a picture of Mom when
>she was young,
>>an empty bottle of beer, an old
>>Railroad spike,
and the head of a hoe with wood still in it
where it broke,
>and a jar of salt for a midnite snack of
>fresh tomatoes.
>A handmade pitchfork Robert made,
>leans on the desk.

~~~~~

We are, Anyway

Such an Autumn day
Sunlight dancing on every leaf   sparkle

Daily Service touching with the Earth

how small we are, with our
    short needs   long needs
thoughts like clouded days
attachments on material levels
        falling glitter
trying to become those Swelled Roots
when in fact, We Are, anyway

The Full Moon,
October First
First October
The Moon Full
Mules outside in the field
cast long shadows   moving

JWL 1974/2019

Fence-lines

Tommy, Frank, Josh and I patched the
fence-line around Morris' hillside.
The woods are truly spectacular. High
wind blowing in rain soon.
Thousands of leaves
dancing gold to the ground,
sound of ocean all around.
Beech, Oak and Maple.

Working on the fence-line thinking:
Who was it drew this first line?
When was it first strung?
And how often has it been repaired?
Barbed wired grown into trees -deep as a
half-a- foot,
Plowshare rusting on the stump of a post...
Ghosts of Fences Past.
We have a gate to build before we end the
day that ends with rain.

When it's real cold.
        When you plow with a team of horses,
    you have to stop now and again to clear the
    plow.
    Break off the row
    clear the plow,
    then, pull it and the team, backwards and
        "back, back team, back"
    the jangle of the trace line chains, wood and
        metal
    and creaking harness leather.
    And your ankles
    and the phfuff from your team
    and the bite from reins across your
        shoulders.

Jack threw a shoe today
   Bob has a barbed wire cut to his leg from
   the day before and he stays home.
Working until "there ain't no more sun"
Unharnessing under lamplight in the barn
where the shadows are big
and dark where the horse shies from the
light
-steps further back in shadow and stomps
the barn floor
Hungry and tired

I have purple hands from the Gentian Violet I use
to care for Bob's leg.

Jwl 1974/2019

Sunday Benedictions

O these October Days – Cold Chill to the Bone
  The First Snow – so very light and so unsure
              Birds sing hesitant

Grey Heavy Thick Clouds
    spread like a blanket from Ridgetop to Ridgetop
              Red noses and Warming hands
      Sunday Benedictions to the Wood Burning Stove

I have noticed the Pleiades in the
northeastern sky
- in the Taurus Constellation
The seven daughters of Atlas and Pleione.

Alcyone - Merope - Celaeno
Taygeta - Maia - Electra - Sterope

Jupiter transformed the sisters into doves,
then into stars to enable them to escape the
attention of Orion.
In another tale, the sisters killed themselves
when Atlas was turned into a mountain.

So the mountain breathes with Autumn
fire
Orion turns his view
The sisters breathe ~ comes winter's air

Essence of Us

Plowing Potatoes with Mules.
Clumsy footwork. Co-ordination and strength.
Watching Potatoes pop out from the earth
between the plowshares and the handles.
Picking them up inside the furrows- some buried –
soft clods.
Some just jumped out as far as a foot from the
row.
Witnessing Excited Tubers.

Pick them up in buckets,
spread them out to dry,
sack them, haul them
to home on the wagon, and the peeler, cookstove
and plate,
down into the damp-deep shadows
to sleep in the underground cellar bins.

Finding Truth in the Brown Furrows and Cropped
Ground
Harrowed Hallowed Land
Swelled Roots to Store for Nourishment

Like Peasant Picture Paintings
All the People were Tanned and Brown too
We are the Ageless Ancients
Essence of us – Peasants on the land

jwl 1974/2019

Orion

Orion can now be seen by 8:30p
The Hunter laying leisurely across the
ridge-line
Seven Sisters whisper and hum
Evenings are colder now – 3 mornings of
heavy frost
– ice glazing sides of the streambanks.
Getting used to fire building in my
little stove –
experimenting with banking
techniques
– so I'll have coals in the morning and
don't wake up cold.
Need another wood-trip tomorrow.

Rooster Stew

Worked on the guitars today, changed
tuning gears, re-strung and polished them.
'Had an idea to refinish an old guitar for
the children and school.

~~~~

Talking with Tom tonight. He said
"we are at the end of a 30 year warm cycle
and the weather is   'Getting back' to the
way it used to be- at least that's what I
read"...
We laughed and went in the house to eat
Rooster Stew.

November First, Nineteen Hundred and Seventy Four

Last night was Halloween – I got the team together, piled hay on the wagon, gathered up our chillun's – drove over to Cremo gathered up the folks there and went for a Hayride under a "less- than" full moon.

I drove there and back, Frank took over at one point, while I sat on the back – played guitar and led the "sing- song".

Magical.

Sunday November 3

      Yesterday was a big Union at the "Feed Corn" Field. We harvested close to half the field. We're all astounded at how much corn we grew and only now realize –
we might not have enough corn crib space. But, we know neighbors can help us out if need be.
           Today I moved the rest of the squash up into my space in the Grain Loft. Now I have a beautiful Squash Carpet- wall to wall.
      It's a quiet and overcast day - people picking up their pieces before they leave for the North.
I feel constant and reassured of this place and it's value.

          ~~~~~

Real strong November winds today –
         temperature remains warm
      Barn Doors slam open
~ the wind sighs over and through the
    buildings
      a taste of sea – storm in a land-locked
    pasture.

SCHOOL HOUSE BLUES

There is a now a definite amount of high energy directed to the school for the kids.. Columbus Day is when classes and the day-care center begin. Today, Judy, Frank Bobby and I began remodeling the Big House to accommodate a classroom experience.

As the plans begin, the downstairs will be pre-school and upstairs will be arts and crafts for the older set.

We are under close observation and criticism by the Townspeople of The System , who do not happen to agree with how we live our lives.

As rumors swell – they are out to make trouble because they have the Laws and Rules they want us to follow.

Friday with Donna at the Woodpile

The grey clouds yesterday brought
rains late today
    and a heavy fog tonight.
It feels unusually warm.
Donna helped me at the wood-pile,
 - gave up on the stinking, noisy and
un-reliable chainsaw
   Switched to the Rhythm Dance of
   the 2 man saw
    We cut about 2 weeks worth.
Went to the Dreamer Farm
   and ate raccoon.

Tuesday night Near full moon

We have begun harvesting the feed corn from Marion's field .
Two wonderful days actually, with Jack, Bob and Dolly and the folks on the detail.
Good "stoop labor" where we ride down home at dark and I blindly unharness everyone, my hands find all the buckles and snaps, scoop the corn and oats, brush them down.
Not too long ago, I learned that Fred Bordell was the man who broke & trained the mules. Would love to meet him. 'Still a lot of corn to harvest.

Wednesday November 6

This morning, Judy, Gideon and Donna left for New York City.

Now, that leaves me, Frank, Yana, Sheila and her boy Masai to hold the farm. Yesterday, a couple with 3 children showed up from Michigan. They heard we were buying up a lot of land and wanted to rent some from us.

Of course that isn't our trip at all, we tried to be hospitable.

She is 21, he is 17 - with 3 children and almost broke and looking for someone to provide for them. We let them stay for 2 days and had to send them on their way.

Godspeed

Sunday November 11

Woke up with a shock. Dolly our Draft Mare
(and my sweetheart)
had fallen over a stream bank, on her right side, the bank was steep enough she essentially pinned herself.
Our neighbor – Harold Metz found her as he was coming back from hunting this morning. She must've been there a good part of the night and would have died if she hadn't been found this morning.
Everyone who was around came down. We tried to pull her out with ropes and eventually brought in the old tractor -
She's a Big girl – I was told by the vet = 14 hands or 60 inches -
floor to withers. No telling how heavy. She's Okay, looks stiff and sore on her right side and she's not limping.
I'm not sure who was shaking more – me or her.
I stayed in the barn with her all day.
It's a blessing it's been kinda warm, I bathed her – she was a muddy mess – covered her in blankets and love
will check on her through the night

Thursday Night in the Big house

Alone all day long.
Worked in the tool shed fixing and sharpening all the axes and the two-man saw.
Rain changed to snow around noon and took a walk up the back holler past the little house.
The woods- truly spectacular with snow drifting down hard.
Each flake making a tapping sound.
Came upon a Buck & Doe – magnificent animals – and fast away from me.
I made tracks towards home, hearth and supper by the wood-stove.

Peaceful.

End Pieces

I left the farm in 1975, travelled back up North to
be with my Dad and family.
1976 found me in Ireland.
I visited the farm in 1977, on my way out west to
Santa Fe.
It was sold in the late 1990's and was turned into a
Hunting Camp.

I retired from the "work-a-day", at the end of
2018.
Living in Lawrence Kansas, I continue writing my
stories, poems
and family histories,
playing the Fiddle, teaching myself Piano and Viola
...and enjoy a Pot-pie of a Wednesday night.

Cheersaye,

himself

jwlyons3249@ gmail.com

At Dad's House – 1974

The All of It

What fine tapestries we weave
with song,
with the tales of days long gone,

and those yet to come.

What fine tapestries we warp and weave and spin
through our children
the gifts we give and to their's the warp, the weave,
and spin as well

A fine rack, rattle, wattle, and weave we make
through living the loves, the dreams,
the real, the challenges, defeats and the lesser
dreams
and the over-comes.

The All of it

jwl 2019

CREDITS

BOOKCOVER – Rowell's Run Farm – 1974

FRONTPEICE – (Whitman) The First Page of the handwritten Journals

BACKPAGE– Johnny at Dad's house – 1974

PUBLISHER – 2-Pups Publishing

EDITING AND TYPE SETTING – Karla Meyer

KOKOPELLI DESIGN– Author/ 2019

TRI-SKELL DESIGN – Teralyn Meyer

www.ingramcontent.com/pod-product-compliance
Lightning Source LLC
Chambersburg PA
CBHW031558040426
42452CB00006B/335